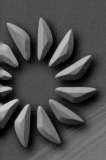

DISCOVER MORAY EELS

by **Kathryn Beaton**

Cherry Lake Publishing • Ann Arbor, Michigan

3

Published in the United States of America
by Cherry Lake Publishing
Ann Arbor, Michigan
www.cherrylakepublishing.com

Content Adviser: Dominique A. Didier, PhD, Associate Professor, Department of Biology, Millersville University
Reading Adviser: Marla Conn, ReadAbility, Inc

Photo Credits: © C.K.Ma/Shutterstock Images, cover; ©Adrian Nunez/Shutterstock Images, 4; © jeffreychin/Shutterstock Images, 6; © Cigdem Sean Cooper/ Shutterstock Images, 8, 10; © serg_dibrova/Shutterstock Images, 12; © Moize nicholas/Shutterstock Images, 14; © Angelo Giampiccolo/Shutterstock Images, 16; © littlesam/Shutterstock Images, 18; © Adam Ke/Shutterstock Images, 20

Library of Congress Cataloging-in-Publication Data
Beaton, Kathryn, author.
  Discover Moray eels / Kathryn Beaton.
    pages cm.—(Splash!)
  Summary: "This Level 3 guided reader introduces basic facts about moray eels, including their physical characteristics, diet, and habitat. Simple callouts ask the student to think in new ways, supporting inquiry-based reading. Additional text features and search tools, including a glossary and an index, help students locate information and learn new words."—Provided by publisher.
  Audience: Ages 6–10
  Audience: K to grade 3
  Includes bibliographical references and index.
  ISBN 978-1-63362-601-0 (hardcover)—ISBN 978-1-63362-691-1 (pbk.)—ISBN 978-1-63362-781-9 (pdf)—ISBN 978-1-63362-871-7 (ebook)
  1. Morays—Juvenile literature. I. Title.

QL638.M875B43 2015
597.43—dc23
                                  2014048640

Cherry Lake Publishing would like to acknowledge the work of the Partnership for 21st Century Skills. Please visit www.p21.org for more information.

Printed in the United States of America
Corporate Graphics

TABLE OF CONTENTS

Snake-Like Fish

Moray eels are long, **muscular** fish. They look like big snakes that can swim. But they are not snakes.

Moray eels have long, snake-like bodies.

Moray eels can be many colors. They are usually dark. Sometimes they have stripes or spots. They do not have **scales** like most fish do.

LOOK!

Look at the pattern on this moray eel. What would be a good name for it? Go online, type in a description, and see if you can find what its real name is.

Some moray eels, like this one, have many different colors and patterns on their bodies.

Male and female eels look almost the same. The females lay eggs in the water. But the parents do not stay to take care of their babies. As they get older, the young eels (called **elvers**) look just like their parents, only smaller.

This elver has grown a lot since its birth.

Underwater Hunters

Moray eels are **carnivorous**. Their strong **jaws** and two sets of sharp teeth help them eat meat. They also have a great sense of smell.

THINK!

Some people keep moray eels as pets. Go online to find out more. What food and other supplies do morays need? Would you ever keep one? Explain why or why not.

This giant moray has good hunting skills.

Moray eels use their sharp teeth and their sense of smell for hunting **prey**. They eat small fish, octopuses, squid, crabs, and other sea creatures. Sometimes they eat other moray eels!

This moray eel has caught a parrotfish.

Moray eels are not **endangered**. There is a big **population** of them all over the world. They can live in warm water and cold water.

This moray eel lives off the coast of French Polynesia, a group of islands in the Pacific Ocean.

Shy and Sneaky

Sometimes **scuba** divers like to look for moray eels. They might feed them. But they need to be careful! Moray eels can bite.

MAKE A GUESS!

A scuba diver might see a moray eel. What are some ways that scuba divers can stay safe?

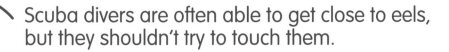

Scuba divers are often able to get close to eels, but they shouldn't try to touch them.

Moray eels are **fierce**, but they are also shy. They like to hide in between big rocks. They live alone.

They look scarier than they really are! Moray eels usually have their mouths open, which shows their sharp teeth. But this is the only way they can breathe. They need to open their mouths so that water can flow in.

Moray eels live by themselves.

Moray eels are sneaky. They stay deep underwater, swimming in secret. There are still many things scientists do not know about these interesting creatures.

We still have a lot to learn about moray eels.

Think About It

Moray eels are strong and can defend themselves. But they try to avoid other animals. Why do you think that is?

Ask your parents or teacher if you can visit an aquarium to see moray eels. Before you go, write down what you think you will see. When you return home, write down what you saw.

Sometimes people cook moray eels to eat. Would you ever try a bite of one? Why or why not?

Find Out More

BOOK

Niver, Heather Moore. *20 Fun Facts about Moray Eels*.
   New York City: Gareth Stevens Publishing, 2013.

WEB SITE

ZooBorns: Baby Moray Eels Are a Worldwide First
www.zooborns.com/zooborns/2014/01/moray-vienna.html
See photos and an article about the first newborn moray eels that scientists have ever been able to study.

Glossary

carnivorous (kahr-NIV-ur-uhs) having meat as a regular part of the diet

elvers (EL-vers) young eels

endangered (en-DAYN-jurd) in danger of dying out

fierce (FEERS) violent or dangerous

jaws (JAWZ) bones around the mouth that have teeth on them

muscular (MUHS-kyuh-lur) having strong muscles

population (pahp-yuh-LAY-shuhn) all of the animals living in a certain place

prey (PRAY) an animal that is hunted by another animal for food

scales (SKAYLZ) thin, hard pieces of skin that cover the body of a fish

scuba (SKOO-buh) underwater swimming with a tank of compressed air on your back that you can breathe through a hose

Index

About the Author

Kathryn Beaton lives and writes in Ann Arbor, Michigan.